22 Thangs Men and Women Should Aught Not Do in Relationships!

Black Mermaid

Published by BookLocker.com, Inc., St. Petersburg, Florida.

Printed on acid-free paper.

BookLocker.com, Inc.
2018

First Edition

DISCLAIMER

This book details the author's personal experiences with and opinions about relationships. The author is not a licensed psychologist.

The author and publisher are providing this book and its contents on an "as is" basis and make no representations or warranties of any kind with respect to this book or its contents. The author and publisher disclaim all such representations and warranties, including for example warranties of merchantability and relationship advice for a particular purpose. In addition, the author and publisher do not represent or warrant that the information accessible via this book is accurate, complete or current.

The statements made about products and services have not been evaluated by the U.S. government. Please consult with your own legal, accounting, medical, or other licensed professional regarding the suggestions and recommendations made in this book.

Except as specifically stated in this book, neither the author or publisher, nor any authors, contributors, or other representatives will be liable for damages arising out of or in connection with the use of this book. This is a comprehensive limitation of liability that applies to all damages of any kind, including (without limitation) compensatory; direct, indirect or consequential damages; loss of data, income or profit; loss of or damage to property and claims of third parties.

You understand that this book is not intended as a substitute for consultation with a licensed medical, legal or accounting professional. Before you begin any change in your lifestyle in any way, you will consult a licensed professional to ensure that you are doing what's best for your situation.

This book provides content related to relationship topics. As such, use of this book implies your acceptance of this disclaimer.

Dedication

This book is dedicated to all single dating men and women looking for a long-term companion or marriage. Keep hope alive; it worked for me!

Contents

Men...

This section, obviously, is for the men. The purpose for you 'actually' reading this is for you to be entertained and enlightened at the same time. Some of you may know many or all of these things but sometimes hearing them comically written from a woman's point of view may have some positive impact. Now understand that I did not just sit down to pour out my negative energy on the man. Unlike many women (as so many men now say), I am *pro-male, pro-husband*! Guys, there are loads of women who feel the same way. That whole, *"I don't need a man"* speech is really a verbal Band-Aid to cover up the wounds many women have received throughout the war and battle of landing a good catch or finding a compatible mate. They don't really mean it. What they really mean is, *"I don't need a man that is going to put me through the things we talk about in your section of this book!"* Let me say that I am very independent but wise enough to know that I *do* need a man! Today's woman is often very independent and self-sufficient. It kind of goes along with the territory of where we are in space and time and what society has evolved into. However, it is Biblically incorrect for a woman to proclaim that she doesn't need a man. If you are an unbeliever, it is illogical. Male and female serve a purpose; both individually and as a couple. Men, you are our covering; our protectors; our leaders; our strong rock. Believe me, most women need *and* want that! If you encounter a woman and she tells you that she doesn't need a man, your response need be: *"So are you androgynous?"* No, I'm kidding. Your response should be, *"Explain to me why not, since we are two different beings and provide*

1

very different things in a relationship?" I guarantee if she has half a brain and you generally seem interested in knowing what her answer is, you will see her actually begin to think about what she said!

All I'm trying to say is, men, we love you, we want you *and* we need you; just not in some of the ways that you have come to believe. The points addressed below derive from conversations that I've had with women. These are some of the general things they complain, and cry about. So, open your mind and your heart because a closed mind cannot absorb and a closed heart cannot love.

Thang Number One:
Never Strike Her

    This topic doesn't really require a long explanation in my opinion. It's quite simple: violence is not an option. This kind of disrespect leads to possible legal problems; in layman's terms: you could end up in jail, dead or ruining your life for good! Striking a woman even once is often the prelude to continuous physical abuse. Physical abuse is disrespect at its extreme. *Never ever* justify putting your hands on a woman. In your defense, some women *really* do take you there! Trust, there are those who will challenge and insight physical fighting; but don't let them! This is a woman who has serious issues because she doesn't even seem to realize that you can and *will* win...nine times out of ten (unless she clocks you with that serious surprise sucker punch or pulls out her equalizer). Walk away and don't look back; no matter how good the punany is. A woman who loves you and who is smart will not put her hands on you. Nobody's goodies are worth death or jail time! Here is where the saying 'women are like buses' is a good motto. Wait for another bus!

Thang Number Two:
Never Lead Her On

Guys, guys, guys! Don't do this. I know that sometimes you may feel desperate (we all do) for attention or sex, but please don't lead a woman on; about anything! If you meet a woman and she is not exactly what you are looking for (which you should already know what you're looking for), then take it for what it is. Be honest; not mean, not insulting; just honest. There is nothing wrong with saying: *"I'm not really feeling you like that, but we could be friends"* or *"I'm not in the market for a long-term commitment but we could hang out sometimes"*. Women say it, don't they? Not so hard to say, fellas; if you just get your head out of your penis! If you are only interested in casual sex, then say so. Don't tell the woman that she's 'the finest thing in the room' just for sex to get your rocks off when you know full well there is a paper bag just the size of her head waiting at your house or you only plan to do it doggy style with the mirrors covered. This is not helpful for you or her. There really is somebody for everybody and if you're not her somebody, then don't pretend to be. This could be a very costly sex session because you have led her to believe that she has a chance in hell with you; when you know she don't! Then when she starts blowing up your phone and texting at all hours you're irritated; and because you're not Ronald Isley, and you don't know how to 'let her down easy', you become rude and resentful. Best to avoid this, my man. Wait for the right fish to come along or be honest and up front so she can make a conscious choice about whether she wants to deal with your menu options. Be an adult!

Thang Number Three:
Never Criticize Her Parents or Children

Tact and diplomacy in a relationship can be very helpful *and* crucial if you don't exercise these qualities when it comes to this very delicate matter. Think about how you would feel if someone criticized your lineage or offspring: you would be livid! Don't think a woman doesn't feel the same. When you criticize a person's parents, it is a direct attack on who they are; even if you're right! Again, tact and diplomacy; and if you don't have either of these qualities: SILENCE! No one wants to hear negative things about their parents even if they are true. If she is doing the criticizing let your words be yea, yea and nay, nay (quoting Scripture now)! By the same token, don't criticize her children. Now I know that some women have birthed the spawn of Chucky, Bay-Bay's Kids or The Bad Seed; but you knew she had kids when you met her (I bet ya did!). And I realize that you were unaware that they were Rosemary's babies; but there is a way to handle this. *Tactfully* and *diplomatically* discuss with her their behavior issues, disrespectful manners and overall wicked ways. If you really like or love this woman, try to help her (God knows she needs it because single parenting is tough)! If she's a good woman she will recognize this and accept your olive branch towards peace and tranquility, because truthfully the kids make *her* sick! But if she is the kind of woman who is blind to the fact or who chooses to wear those rose-colored glasses when it comes to her bad a** children; my man, YOU have a choice! She doesn't. They are her responsibility (unless you fathered one, then that's another topic) and not yours. Believe me, you do not want to come between a woman and her children because if she lets you: she ain't worth the high heels she's sporting... and if she doesn't let you: you will end up inciting the wrath of Khan! Remember: you hold the big joker in this case; be smooth: exit, stage left!

Thang Number Four:
Never Belittle Her

You know how they say, *"You get more with honey than vinegar"?* Well this is what *they* meant. We talked about criticism in the previous section, but direct criticism is also a no, no! Women naturally want to be beautiful because it's pleasing to a man; we all do. Unfortunately, we all aren't! Some of us are shaped funny, (too big up top or bottom; or not big enough up top or bottom) got left out when God passed out hair, showcase skinny legs; have bad skin; bare stretch marks from fat or pregnancy; you name it, we got it. There is no such thing as a physically perfect woman (*I said there isn't*- Halle Berry is not perfect either!). But a smart man can make that woman perfect for him. Enhance what she has and help her fix what she doesn't. She will love your dirty drawers for it! Don't talk about her or dog her verbally (or physically, for that matter; see **"Thang Number One"**) about her less than perfect looks and imperfections. She wants to feel she is beautiful to you and if she loves you, she will do her best to make that happen and you should *help* her. If she's too fat, get a gym membership together. If she's bald, get her a weave or a wig. If her legs are skinny, tell her how much you love to see her in those sexy <u>long</u> skirts (she will go out and buy them all). If she has no boobs, take her to Vicky's Secrets and get her a padded push up bra (or if you got deep pockets, breast implants). If she has bad skin, take her to Mac and explore skin care products. But for God's sake don't make her feel worse by dragging her through the mud with insalubrious words. Words hurt and create scars that don't heal. Don't make your woman scornful, resentful or to the point where she just gives up and doesn't care anymore. You'll be in for a real treat then...

Thang Number Five:
Never Give Her Everything

As we previously discussed not to belittle a woman, it is equally important to never give her everything. Listen gentleman, here are a couple of good reasons why it's not a good idea to do this.

When you give a woman everything it shows that you are insecure and weak. Now, as women, we may not know *why* you are insecure or *what* you are insecure about; but it definitely sends off a negative signal. This in turn, depending on what kind of woman you are dealing with, will cause your partner to do one of two things: leave you abruptly (or eventually) or go into full blown 'use you' mode. That's right! You *too* can be used! This is how you fall into things like buying your way into her heart, calling all the time to see if she is still yours, assuming that every man breathing wants her, and changing into a proverbial Renfield. This is not a good look; to the fellas OR other women! It tends to make women see you as 'less manly', inadequate and incapable. Incapable of what, you ask? Incapable of loving correctly and efficiently. If you come across to a woman as a pushover, this is not a challenge for her. Yes, women like a little challenge as well. She *wants* to have to work a wee bit to get and keep your attention or she will conclude that she does not have to put forth any efforts to show her worth. She will also conclude that you don't love yourself and you have low self-esteem; so how could you possibly know how to love her? Now, a good woman will excuse herself from your presence gracefully and offer you a cordial reason as to why she is not interested. However, a sinister sister (no race specified) will take the bags and run; frequently returning for even more bags! This scenario is not to support the notion that 'women like thugs and bad boys', as so many men seem to think (even though I admit, some do). However, it affirms the fact that undeserved spoiling will lead to emotional and financial disaster just as it does with children. Believe me, a woman *must* feel that she has a man and not an 'Elmo' (as in puppet for those of you who are unfamiliar). A man must be strong and robust, yet kind and giving. I know it's confusing and frustrating to some of you, so I'll provide a few examples. It's cool to take a woman out shopping if you have bided enough time with her (this is not an 'out of the gate' thang to do). But when you go shopping, set some limitations in the beginning (whether you can afford it or not). Buy her something nice like a jacket, a pair of jeans, a watch or an anklet; not a pair of diamond earrings, a ring, red bottom shoes or a Coach bag. Even if you have deep pockets and can afford it and she knows it, she will feel that you see your finances as your number one trait. Learn to execute simple dates like walks in the park, picnics, museums and stuff like that. This will give her the impression that you are a man of character substance and not simply financial means. Bottom line: it will make her respect *yo* money! Women love attention (most of them) and if they seem annoyed by your attention giving, that is a clear sign that she either doesn't like you or already has someone else that she's set her heart on. Don't waste your time! If she likes you the occasional 'free' dates, thought provoking gifts and simply your time and attention will win her over faster than any over-the-limit credit card you could pull out of your wallet. This is not a ticket to be cheap; that's something very different. Be innovative; use the Internet to gather ideas. But don't use your money cause in the end, you'll lose that honey; "... can't by you love!" P.S. again, this section does not apply to skanks!

Thang Number Six:
Never Make Promises You Can't Keep

Y'all be drooling over Baby Face's and Luther's sappy lyrics but as Dru Hill sang: *"...never make a promise that I can't keep"*. Aside from the fact that this is rude and cruel, you don't need to make promises that you have no intentions on keeping; nor could you even if you wanted to. I always wondered about those love songs that promise 'the sun, the moon and the stars'. It sounds good but how are you going to give me something that doesn't even belong to you? S-T-O-P! You don't need to promise a woman stuff that you can't deliver – number one. Now if she is requesting things that she *knows* you can't afford, uh, please refer back to the end of the paragraph of **"Thang Number Five"**: again, this section does not apply to skanks! No self-respecting woman is going to ask her man who works at Burger King (part time) to take her to Paris. *Really?* So, your nose is that far open that you tell her you're going to make this happen? You need Jesus and a reality check! We won't even go there again; re-read the previous section. However, *simple* things are just as heart breaking. Don't tell a woman that you are going to call her at nine when you get off from work and she doesn't hear from you until the next morning cause you ran into 'Pookie and Them' and they wanted to play a quick game of Grand Theft Auto and you just 'forgot'. Not acceptable! At the very least, go into the bathroom and call her (cause I know you don't want 'Pookie and Them' to hear you) and give her an honest explanation. Talk with her for at least 15 to 20 minutes. Ask her about her day and how she is doing and make plans for the next time you will see her and let her know what you plan to do to her when you do (give her something to think about). This emotional Vic Salve will heal that unexpected prick to her heart you gave by not reserving 'her phone call time' (as she took it to mean) when you said you'd call after work. And as for 'Pookie and Them', flush the toilet a couple of times and tell them you had a slight case of the bubble guts (you *do* work at Burger King). All I'm saying is: FOLLOW THROUGH! It is important to follow through at all costs, if it comes out of your mouth! Women are like walking computers when it comes to storing information. We store words (document files) and actions (video files); and the accuracy is uncanny! So again, FOLLOW THROUGH! If you say you're going to call; call. If you say you're going to come by; stop by. If you say at 8 o'clock, be there at 7:55. If for some reason you can't keep your promise (cause for us, they are all promises) then you need to do better than 'I forgot' or just not addressing it at all. This is a road map to driving a woman to Scornful Land USA. And she may put up with this foolishness for a while, depending on how much she cares for you, but please believe it: your redemption draws nigh! Repetitive disappointments equal dangerous imaginations for a woman. You *could not* be cheating, but in her mind, you are. And one of the hardest scriptures for a woman to obey is Romans 12:19, *"Dearly beloved, avenge not yourselves, but rather give place unto wrath: for it **is** written, **Vengeance is mine**; I will repay, saith the Lord."* So be considerate, guys. It's a quality that women <u>cherish</u>!

Thang Number Seven:
Never Joke about Marriage

Perhaps this is the BEST follow up to the previous section dealing with broken promises. Ah, marriage: the thing that most women seem to anticipate and the thing that most men seem to belate! From the beginning of childhood, the value of marriage and landing a good man is instilled in our heads. All the fairy tales spoke of it: Cinderella, Snow White, Rapunzel; all lucky women, beautiful and fair, who wound up living happily ever after with a handsome man who came and rescued them from utter despair. Ask any woman and she knows the story – verbatim – of these famous and fortunate women. How could a girl not dream of this? And I note again: *the handsome man came to rescue them.* Guys, most every time you make your acquaintance with a woman and you meet a minimum of five of her 'ideal standards' for her mate, you become her potential Prince Charming; if she's hoping for marriage. Now, I know you didn't apply for the position nor did you choose to be a candidate, but this is what is brewing in a woman's head; and this does not include the desperate ones! Let's face it: men are taught to frolic and women are taught to be the flowers in the field they frolic through. In all fairness to men, all of you are not ready to be married (nor are you marriage material, to tell the truth); and for women, most of us do have standards we adhere to as well (don't think we just want any ol' Joe). But if you are not ready, not thinking of, not willing to, not able to, not capable of (already married, gay or a eunuch), then DO NOT, I repeat **DO NOT** mention marriage, joke about it, or toy with the idea in her presence. FOUL BALL! We women will perceive your words and/or actions as *"This must be him, girl!"* Call us what you want, but it's the truth. And when that doesn't happen...OH the emotional devastation that can occur. I know you think I'm gassing up this topic but, believe me, I'm not. It's best to not even bring it up if you are not sure or not emotionally there at all. Never say things like: *"Girl, you can cook yo a** off; Imma have to marry you!"* or *"Baby, you know how to put it on me; I need to put a ring on it because that thang has gots to be mine!"* Lines like these infer marriage for real in a woman's mind. And if she's feeling you like that, you have planted that seed in her heart AND her head. The next thing you know, she'll be asking you questions about it and throwing you hints. Then you become annoyed and label her as clingy and desperate. News flash, fellows: *"Marriage **is** honorable in all, and **the bed is undefiled**: but whoremongers and adulterers God will judge"* (Hebrews 13:4; aw shut up! Some of y'all need some church in your lives). And for all you unbelievers, *"Why buy the cow when you can get the milk for free?"* Bottom line is, no self-respecting woman wants to be your bed wench for an extended period of time. And if she is spiritual, she definitely doesn't want to be a 'whoremonger' or an 'adulterer' (cause some of y'all already married and throwing out idle hints). Anita Baker sang, *"...reality steps into view; no longer living life in paradise...no fairy tales!"* (You know the lyrics; it's deep!) This is **cardinal rule**, men; no laughing matter to a woman at all. You know how you don't like jokes about your manhood...? Point taken!

Thang Number Eight:
Never Assume Your
Sexual Skills are Stellar

This is a VERY sensitive topic for men, especially since they all seem to feel that they are Don Juan, Casanova and Rudolph Valentino all rolled into one! This **"Thang"** is so special that I will need to break it down into smaller categories to make myself crystal clear. No more delay; let's start with "The Task Master".

"The Task Master" is a 'man's man'. He feels that since he is physically deemed a man that he automatically knows what a woman wants more than *she* does. He knows how to please her simply because at birth he grew gonads instead of a vagina in the fourth month of gestation; and he is utterly insulted by sex toys. So, he never bothers to ask her what she wants, or likes, for that matter. Women compare him to a rooster because he usually gets on top and is about his business for as long as it takes for *him* to climax (usually averaging anywhere from 1 to 3 seconds) and then his job is complete. If his partner protests, she is being ungrateful and unreasonable *"because no one else ever complained before"*. Truth is, he didn't listen to *them* either. He is convinced it is her fault that she didn't climax therefore, something is obviously wrong with her.

"The Marathon Man" is proud that he has the stamina and strength of a bull. However, he has the brains of a Dung Beatle because he doesn't know when to say when. Pounding on a woman for endless hours does not make you a Dr. of Dickology. It does not mean you are 'putting it down' or 'laying pipe'. It does, however, make a woman very bored and sore if she is feeling anything less than enjoyment. When the level of dryness seems to increase with each stroke, that woman has lost interest no matter how much she moans in ecstasy (shame on you fakers; please refer to your chapter). Believe me, this gives 'dry humping' a WHOLE new meaning; and it ain't always her fault that the faucet turned off!

"The Circus Freak" is the man who wants to do any and everything his pea brain can conjure up to do to you. He appears to believe that you feel absolutely no pain; you are a human voodoo doll and can take every convoluted idea that crosses his mind. So, he suggests positions that would require you to be a contortionist, asks you to allow him to try penetrating your ear lobe or finds contaminated objects in his tool box to replace his 'tool'. Experimenting can be fun, but it can also be deadly. So, leave your lab coat at Party City when it comes to your sex partner, please. This man will make great use of your medical benefits when it comes to seeing your GYN.

"The Party Prude" seems to have been a monk in his former life. He doesn't want to do anything different: EVER; and is quite the opposite of "The Circus Freak". He is the man whose electric bill will never peak because he wouldn't think of turning on the lights during sex or plugging in your favorite toy. Bath tubs are for bathing and tables are for eating. You can always count on 9 o'clock just after his favorite show goes off on Saturday night. Don't bother buying any 'sleazy' lingerie or you'll be labeled the 'Whore of Babylon'. You'd better not initiate sex either; that's his job. He has to be up early for church so don't you dare try to deviate from the regularly scheduled sex program. Besides, he couldn't imagine being burdened with the thoughts of the *sinful* things y'all did the night before during Sunday service!

"The Nice Nasty Neanderthal" is the refined and educated man who seemed to skip the classes on gender equality when he was perusing his degree. In his mind the vagina is simply an object, that he as a man, has the right to insert his penis into; save nothing else. Sex is merely for procreation and a woman doesn't have to enjoy it but endure it. There is no foreplay or intimate touching or kissing going on in his prelude to sex. You must be ready whenever he is because it is your 'Godly duty' since you are merely a woman. If you refuse, it is his Biblical right to find someone who will not refuse him; married or not. It would be his lifelong dream to be able to legally crack a woman over the head with his club, drag her into the bedroom, do his business, impregnate her and send her out to finish the chores so he can take his much-needed nap. When he awakes, he will surely start up his 'Flintstone mobile' to make his way to the strip to pick up a hooker for dessert. Please keep an in-house HIV test available at all times!

These are merely some examples of male lover styles that should be banished forever! Perhaps this is a good reason to get to know more about a woman before you start sniffing her underwear. You will be more comfortable about asking what she likes as opposed to putting yourself in an awkward moment that *commands* that you know what she likes and how to please her. That's WAY too much pressure for anyone. If you're too shy to ask her; ask your sister, ask your co-worker, ask your high school female best friend, ask Ann Landers or Dr. Phil! Just ask somebody! Try going to the library to borrow some books. Knowledge is power! It is also sexy. I know that some women are ancient and stoic and they themselves find it difficult to discuss the details of intimacy, but one of the Ten Commandments of Love is: *Know Thy Partner's Body.* Make the effort men; most women will jump on the bandwagon with you and appreciate you so much more! And the sex...will be unforgettable!

Thang Number Nine:
Never Make Comparisons

Make love, make money, make cookies, make time, but never make comparisons of your partner to another woman! Dude, women are already extremely self-critical, and we are very critical of other women as well. We are hard on each other! If a woman has a hair out of place, we are judging. If a woman is not shapely, we are judging. If a woman has less than perfect teeth, believe me, WE ARE JUDGING! Women are very unforgiving when it comes to other women; but this is an unspoken rule among women. This is what *we* do. We can take it from each other because it is expected. However, from you, we cannot take it! Don't talk about some woman from down the street and how she wears the sexiest shoes you've ever seen. Translation to your woman: *her* shoes are orthopedic, and she has bad taste. Don't talk about how well-spoken your co-worker is or how smart she is. Translation to your woman: *her* communication is poor, and she is stupid. Now I know you're saying, *"So I can't pay another woman a compliment?"* That is not the point here, fellas. You *can* pay another woman a compliment. It just depends on how you do it. For example, you might say, *"Ms. Jones really does wears some sexy shoes each time I see her, but your legs are way sexier. I wish you were more into heels, you would look so much better in them than her!"* See the difference? See how that fosters inspiration and offers suggestion to your partner but at the same time allows you to admire another woman? Try this one: *"My co-worker Jane is ultra-smart and very good with words, but she hasn't got a clue about cooking the way you do, and everyone knows the way to a man's heart is his stomach!"* Translation to your woman: her education may not be comparable to Jane's but that ain't your thang anyway because you love to eat, and she is providing that for you very well!

Ok, now you get the idea how, so let me tell you why. It is the same concept that men harbor: we want to be the best you ever had in all facets (even if we know that isn't true). C'mon men, you know full well y'all feel the same way! You wanna be the first, you wanna be the last, you wanna be her everything! Well guess what? So do we! We want to be the best cook, the best lover, the best looking, the best dresser, the best shaped woman you've ever had. I'd be lying if I said we didn't secretly know that we couldn't possibly cover all that ground. That would be the perfect woman (please see **"Thang Number Four"**); but we want to feel that we are, even when we know we are not. When you say things like, *"My ex made the best lasagna ever!"* Don't look for us to be making lasagna for you anytime too soon because in our minds, what's the use? Ours could never compare to your ex's! That's right, *compare*. You see, if there is no validation of your partner at the beginning or end of your statement it then becomes a direct comparison or indirect criticism! The reason why you don't want that to happen is that you won't get lasagna anymore or a host of *other* things either... I might also mention that the only woman that is exempt from this rule is your mother. You can say that your mother was the best this and that, but I warn you, even mom has an expiration date on the can of compliments. It is a <u>perishable</u> item. Revenge is a dish best served cold; and long after you've been bumping your gums about your mother, sister, Ms. Jones and whomever else, her recipe booklet will be full of 'cold dishes to be served' on a frequent basis and you will not have a clue as to why...

Thang Number Ten:
Never Use Control Tactics

Now listen here, you prison warden, if you want to train and control something buy a dog! They are really the only creature that seem to succumb to such Homo habilis behavior. We all know that control in a relationship could breed many things, but I tell you what it will definitely breed: emotional barriers and distance.

You must learn to trust your partner and allow them to do things by their own resolve and not because you constantly yank on their leash. If you can't trust your partner, then why are you with them in the first place? This is something you must ask yourself. My mother always told me: *"The Bible says, "To the pure all things are pure!""* Well understood when someone is always accusing you and pointing fingers as an excuse to execute 'house arrest'. Think about it like this: if your woman is dating you or committed to you, it most likely is because she really *wants* to be there. So, you do not need to use *Saw* torture tactics to make her stay! However, if you do resort to this (cause I know you didn't display this behavior at the beginning or she would never have locked down with you in the first place — no pun intended) her emotional attachment and love will slowly and eventually fade and so will she!

Control tactics come in many forms: striking (which we've previously condemned), money, sex, affection; those are just some of the most popular ones. However, it doesn't matter which one you use, you will most certainly gain the same result — abandonment! God the creator fashioned us in such a way that we exist and feel the

23

same as He does. And hadn't you noticed (that is, if you're a believer) that He never makes anyone do anything. That would be called Witchcraft: the use of manipulation or supernatural powers to influence persons or events. Yes, I said it! (Don't put the book down now!) Exerting control over your mate is ungodly. Now again, if you are an unbeliever, even good witches are mindful of what spells they cast so as to not over step their bounds. Besides, if a person wants to do something, they will find a way to do it come hell or high water. You are wasting your time and energy. Bottom line, control does not belong in a relationship; it belongs in your hands when you want to change the television channel.

Thang Number Eleven:
Never Disrespect Her

We've already mentioned the ultimate disrespect in **"Thang Number One"**. However, guys, there are a plethora of ways you can disrespect a woman without ever hitting her and sometimes that pain is even worse. Words AND actions do hurt, my man! Let's take a look at some of the classic ways you guys inflict pain on women.

Don't shake your head because you know it's coming: calling a woman a bi**h! Whew! I said it, and I have chills just thinking of it! Now, I do realize that things have changed, and the new Millennium generation uses the term 'bi**h' in a much friendlier way than they did back in my day. Back in my day (and in this day, if you wanna know the truth about it), 'bi**h' is a fight out the gate! Whether a man referred to you as a bi**h or a woman, it meant the fight was on and poppin! Now-a-days, young women call each other bi**h as a generic pet name or term of endearment. Please note: I am <u>not</u> from that school of thought so, please do not refer to me as a bi**h. However, even the newfangled generation who have come to accept this word and not be so offended by it, knows the difference between 'bi**h' as in my girl and 'bi**h' as in derogatory female dog. Say it in anger and you will see that the fight will STILL be on! Men shouldn't call women bi**h even if they behave like one. Why bother? Just let her be who she is and leave her alone. Why would you want to be with a woman that you feel the need to call a bi**h? And besides, you would have a fit if someone called your mother or sister a bi**h, now wouldn't you? Even if they deserved it! The 'bi**h' word just feels so low and dirty to a woman; at least a woman of standards. So, guys, refrain from calling a woman bi**h. I mean, for goodness sakes, you gave your dog a name; you don't call her bi**h!

Mushing a woman's face is so close to striking her I won't even elaborate so much. Keep your hands to yourself, please! She is not your child. She already knows that you're stronger and mushing her face just reaffirms what she already despises: that she can't whoop yo a**. Ok, enough said.

Not introducing her in public is a stinky one. If you are out in public with a woman and you run into a friend, your mom, your ex, or whomever, pre-determine in your mind before your excursion how you will introduce her. I'd advise you *not* to wait until the moment arises because you will be caught off guard and will NOT have a clue as to what you should say. This usually resorts to you just ignoring the situation altogether which is WAY worse. Now, you've ignored her presence. Please don't expect 'dessert' when you take her home. If the woman you are with is not your girlfriend, just introduce her as your friend (old school men call it: lady friend). If you have been dating for a while but not quite sure if she's a girlfriend yet, introduce her as 'your special friend'. Remember to look at her and smile when you say it to add emphasis. She'll like that! If you have girlfriend/boyfriend status, then follow the status quo. It's not really that hard, guys. But I beg you not to choke up and neglect to introduce at all or not include the descriptive adjective in front of her name. Nope! You can't just say, *"This is Shelly."* Now, in her mind, *"Oh, so I'm just Shelly, huh?"* However, if this is a first or second date, a simple first name will suffice. But it better not be the third date out on the town with time spent together in between (her place or yours) and you don't add that distinctive adjective in front of Shelly. The sour face will come, then the silence and you won't even know why. Well I'm telling you why. It's important, but don't go overboard because you'll be kicking yourself if you do. She will hear something totally different (**"Thang Number Seven"**). If you're not sure, talk it out with a friend before the date happens. Every play production goes through a dress rehearsal before it hits Broadway!

Women...

This section, obviously, is for the women. Now don't think for one moment, women, that I will be lax with you. Yes, I wanted to tell the men a thing or two about themselves. However, it's YOU that I want to speak to as well. Women (including myself) always tend to find themselves whining about what a man did, does, or won't do. This is the topic at church meetings, bridal showers, clubs, beauty shops, nail salons, grocery stores...uh, you get my point. We are always complaining about men! Some of us complain with good reason, and others complain just because that's what is going on in their presence and if they say something nice about their man other women will look at them like they are the Benedict Arnold of romance. *Never* be afraid to stand up for your man (when it's right)! Don't get me wrong, the complaining is what prompted me to embark on this project. In fact, one of my friends suggested I do it during one of *our* complaining sessions. So, get your hand off your hip, please. No one said that some things aren't valid. And just like women, guys talk too! Oh yes, they do! Sometimes *way* more than women do. They are always bumpin' their gums at the barber shop, the basketball court, the mechanic garage, the gym and any other place men gather in their caves to marvel at women and try to figure out 'what's wrong with us'. Instead of asking other women, they ask other men (as if they have the answer). So now, back to you. We women have got to realize the power we possess on the inside. This is God-given power and most of us haven't tapped into it nearly as much as we should or are able to do. Have you ever heard men say, *"You just don't know how much power you have."* Well, honey, they mean that! We really don't! They realize their strengths, but they also realize their weaknesses as well. We have no clue, many times, wherein lies our strength. No, I'm not just talking about sex and definitely not talking about manipulation. I'm talking about power within yourself. Stop complaining about there not being 'enough men'. There are plenty! You just haven't uncovered the whole stock! And in order to do this, you must first regain your power and inner strength. Therein lies your answer. So, open your mind, and your hearts and get your hands off your hips because deep inside...you know I'm telling you the truth.

Thang Number One:
Never Use Sex to Get a Man

What? Are you serious? First of all, let me tell you that you are now living in the 21st century. It was during the 20th century (around the early 1900's and prior, in fact) that female virgins were the norm and expected. Now I didn't say there was anything wrong with being a virgin. If you are, God bless you! You are truly a "virtuous woman". However, if you are not, it doesn't constitute a bleeding heart either. This reminds me of a story (one of my own). I was in one of my complaining modes and my dear mother said to me, *"If you stop sleeping with a man, then he will marry you."* Now, I didn't know whether or not to laugh in her face or shake my head in pity at her. Naturally, this was her advice because she was born in the 1930's. This is a time when women were *not* sexually free and were expected to be virgins (hence the white wedding dress and all). It was customary for a man to 'court' a young lady. Women didn't generally work outside the home and men were suitors that would provide food, shelter and children if her womb was blessed to create a family to carry on his surname. Boom! That blew up for real in the 70's and women have been progressively sexually free ever since!

Now having said all that, in this day and age, not having sex with your partner is a sure way to accomplish a few things. One, he will inevitably go find it elsewhere. Two, he *will* marry you just to get the sex. And three, he will go find it elsewhere and not come back. Being pious is a beautiful and righteous thing to do. So, I'm **not** advising anyone against this. What I will say, though, is if this is how you want to conduct yourself, do it from the start and do it because these are your values no matter what. You must do it from the beginning because if you start feeding a dog from the table then he will expect table food! (No, men, I am not referring to you as dogs! It's just an analogy.) If this is how you choose to conduct your life, then let your suitor know up front that you are and intend to remain celibate until marriage – no compromise! Because if you *do* compromise and give in (and he will test you) you lose leverage AND respect. Remember: word is bond! Now indeed if you love and respect your body and the Word of God in your plight of celibacy, again, this is a beautiful thing and an honorable choice. However, if you are wagging your tongue about being celibate because "no one deserves your great cookies" or "he is gonna have to pay to get these goodies", then YOU, honey boo-boo, are sadly mistaken and misinformed! Remember the line in the movie, *The Best Man*: "...Ain't nothin better than some p**** except some new p****!" Uh, fiction breathes life, ladies. Please believe it! Yours is *not* better, than the next. They did not break the mold after *your* vroom box. Sure, you might know a few extra tricks and moves but it is **very** dangerous to use this in manipulation tactics when trying to get a man's attention and keep it! (OMG, how long is this chapter?) Long enough to try to get you to see that the sex game is played!!! There are too many other options. Men do not have to solicit prostitutes in order to achieve 'free' sex anymore. They do not have to settle for your sex manipulation 101 course. Don't be a fool ALL your life! Men don't like games and *this* one probably irritates them the most! Be a grown woman. If you choose to have sex with a partner, then be grown about your stuff and do it. Don't worry about who thinks what. That's decisive and confident. I didn't say sleep with everyone (as that's an entirely different subject). And speaking of which, sexing the man 24 hours a day, 7 days a week utilizing every God-given hole you possess won't work either! (I told you I was going hard on y'all). All things in moderation, honesty and purity of heart. Bottom line: DO NOT use sex (or the lack thereof) to try to get or keep a man. You're not being honest with them or yourself. You'll end up looking and feeling like a fool. And most likely...manless.

Thang Number Two:
Never Physically Challenge Him

Ladies, we've all been there and experienced being angry with a man. Whether it's because he's cheated with someone(s), lied about something (or nothing), said something downright ignorant or insensitive, broke a promise unapologetically, or a host of any other reasons you can think of or have been told by other females. Some of these crimes seem (and sometimes are) punishable by violent physical contact. Whack! That's the sound you hear in your head and the visual you get of your hand (or fist, depending on who taught you to fight) connecting with his face. I get it! I myself have wanted to take on a few of my past contenders as sparing partners out of anger and sheer disappointment. However, DON'T DO IT!

Back in the same era we discussed in the previous chapter, women seemed to have been given a 'pass' to express their insult and pain with applying the *"well I never"* slap to a man's face. Again, this is not that day and time! I wouldn't advise you to put your hand on a man (or another person, for that matter). Before you make that move, you need to consider a few things. 1) You wouldn't want *or* accept a man hitting you no matter how smart you got or how challenging you became. You would be apt to call the police if that happened. I know you're saying, *"But that's different; they hit harder and a man isn't supposed to hit a woman."* Oh no, my friend, that doesn't apply to *all* women. Some of us pack a mean punch! The bottom line is that you have no *right* to be physically violent with anyone — including your man! He is grown and not a child. You cannot discipline him with violence. It will not work. If he's a good man, he will walk away and not be bothered with you again (see the Man's section, **"Thang Number One"**) but if he's 'human', he may forget (having a temporary lapse of the recollection of who you are because of your strike) and open up a can of whoop a** on you. Then you are hurt and embarrassed when you show up with your eye dotted. Keep your hands to yourself and stop watching Turner Classic Network movies because they will get you in a world of trouble. 2) In this day and time (when women have fought *so hard* for equal opportunity), men and society have incorporated this equal favor in every aspect; including domestic violence. Sweetie, you too can go to jail! That's right, he can opt to call the police, and have you locked up for domestic violence. And many men do! If this happens, you *will* get a really good picture of just what 'equal opportunity' means.

I need you to understand that no matter how many marches and protests and voting that has gone on in the past and the present, WOMEN ARE NOT EQUAL TO MEN! I know y'all are upset at that statement, but we *are not*. Call me what you will, but that notion is *not* Biblical nor is it logical. I spoke about realizing your strengths and weaknesses in the introduction to your section. Here is a good point to start re-thinking your existence as a woman...a lady. I'm all for certain things being equal (and that would probably be a whole other book), but in reference to this topic: you need to recognize! You are not physically stronger than a man (unless you're dating Wee Man from Jackass and don't underestimate him either just because he's a Little Person). Physical strength is a God-given attribute to men; given for a reason. We as women have often laughed at the notion 'if men could have babies'. That's because we know they couldn't nor *would* they even if they physically could! I need you to draw from this analogy to get my drift. Use the strengths that God gave you! Oh, you don't know? How about the ability to reason, negotiate and operate with patience? Oh yea, it's hard, but it's smart and honorable!

Don't physically challenge a man, you won't win. And isn't the object of the quarrel to win? Instead, dig deep into your emotions for therein lies *your* strength. Believe me, you will come up with a solution that's way more profitable than a physical challenge. And that's better than coming up with a black eye and spending $100 on a month's worth of MAC concealer...while wearing your new 'Chanel' bracelets and orange jumpsuit! Remember: there should be no 'laying on of hands' in a relationship except for praying and intimate playing.

Thang Number Three:
Never Give Him All

Right out the gate, there is but one you should give your all to: Jesus! And if you're not a spiritual or religious person: yourself! Absolutely! *Never* give a man your all. Now calm down. I'm not referring to putting your best foot forward in your dating endeavors and especially your marriage (it's your duty to do so). You should always try to give your best in these situations but hear me: giving your *best* is not synonymous with giving your *all*. There is grave danger in making this mistake. As I advised the men in their section of **"Thang Number Five"**, never give everything! You must keep something for yourself. No one wants a door mat(e). Where is the challenge? Where is the surprise? If you give everything, you'll have nothing left to give, he will have nothing left to take and then 'futile' replaces 'friendship'. God doesn't give us everything because we wouldn't appreciate those things or Him! Same concept (I told you we were made in His image). If you encounter a man who asks you for any and everything: run! No real man would ask or even want his woman to give him everything. We as women are natural givers and therefore must be careful about nothing when it comes to this. Face it: we want to give, especially when we love. This is one of the beautiful things about being a woman. But don't let this God given beauty become the tragedy of your life. He doesn't need all that! It's not your job to buy and pay for everything, say 'yes' every time he wants to have sex and whatever way he wants to (even when you're not feeling it), give into his every whim and everything beyond that. It's not your job! *"But I will lose him!"* You whine...How about you will not only lose him if you do, but most importantly, you will lose yourself! All things in moderation ladies. It's ok to say no sometimes. And you don't have to say it nastily or with an attitude. Tact is the key. If you aren't feeling something or agreeing with him, just simply say, *"I don't think so, babe."* Sure, he may not like it. He may be angry. Heck! He might even leave you! But if he does, was he worth it in the first place? Nah, I don't think so. So, all those love songs that croon about wanting your "mind, body, and soul", take it for a grain of salt. Because nobody, but NOBODY gets that but...G-O-D!

Thang Number Four:
Never Accuse Him

We women are born lawyers. We can naturally interrogate and mentally manipulate like you wouldn't believe! We have instinct; we can sense and smell everything; Blood Hounds at best. Listen ladies: learn to handle this talent and use it skillfully and only when necessary. No man wants to be accused, interrogated or mentally manipulated. Sometimes we can't help it. It just comes naturally to us. This is a game they cannot win. "We are the champions, my friend"! But consistent accusations and interrogations will eventually lead to a T.K.O. - of your relationship. I know that some men incite this behavior with the nonchalant answers and facial expressions they give. Men generally do not lie very well, and they have no poker face whatsoever. Women, there are ways of interrogating without accusing. You don't say to your man when he comes in at 3 am, *"I know you was with Sonya! Now lemme smell your underwear!"* Ewww! Really? What is that going to accomplish anyway if he was with Sonya? Do you really want the essence of Sonya on the tip of your nose? I don't think so! Here's one: *"Why you lying? I know you were talking to Renee on the phone just now! Lemme see your phone!"* Ladies, don't get me wrong, I've been there; and this is why I can tell you – WRONG MOVE!! First of all, this will only further upset you when he 1.) doesn't comply with your request; 2.) doesn't admit to your accusation; or 3.) mocks you. (That last one makes you want to take out your equalizer fa sho! Uh, no! Please re-read **"Thang Number Two"**.) I've been there too, ladies, and the hurt and humiliation is unforgettable. But you must use your brain and breathe...! Listen, you really don't even need to go into all those accusations because you already know the answer; especially if this isn't the first time. (You showl do!) Set some boundaries for yourself...respect yo self! If this man has already displayed this behavior once before and you find yourself having to address it yet again, just leave! That is the best thing you could do for yourself and him. Leave! Cut your losses and move on. Why stay? He's going to do it again. Lawyers don't keep re-trying the same case over and over. Execute your judgement and be out! This type of man is merely showing you where his heart and his priorities are – and it's not with you! Remember: *he* loses, you don't. Have some dignity. God will send you someone else; or if you're impatient, go find someone else! Don't remain in the situation and keep allowing him to repeat the same behavior. He will not respect you; EVER! Now, for those of you who accuse with no reason, save for pure insecurity, *you* are a relationship killer! If your man comes in at 3 am and this is unacceptable to you, simply grit your teeth and say, *"I don't think you would like it if I came in at 3 am. Do not do it to me. I will not accept it."* And don't! As I stated before, word is bond! If you tell a man you won't go for something, DO NOT give him a pass if he 'tries' you and does it again! But ladies, on the other hand, some men aren't doing anything wrong. And because you have insecurity issues because you aren't as pretty or shapely as his last fling, that's not his problem! He could have had a flat tire or had to stop by to remove the trash he promised his mom he would get earlier that day. Get a grip, AND a clue. If you constantly accuse someone of something, eventually just like Disney, all your dreams will come true! (And eventually become nightmares!) No one, but NO ONE wants to face constant accusations. It leads to the old adage: *"Well I might as well do it, since she insists that I am!"*

Thang Number Five:
Never Tell your Girlfriends/ Mother/Sister Everything

We women our SO expressive and emotional. And as I mentioned in the previous chapter, these are fascinating and very useful traits that God bestowed upon us. We tend to want to verbally express ourselves; especially when emotion plays a large role in the motive for that expression. We analyze, we rationalize, we trivialize; we THINK and therefore we TALK. Talking is a great way to find solutions, discover new ideas AND ruin a PERFECTLY GOOD RELATIONSHIP! Let me explain...

I once had what I called a "Hen Club Party". Yes, I took what we women see as a derogatory term and turned it into a female celebration of ourselves loaded with food, drinks, communication and fun! (You can borrow the idea if you want.) It's good to get with other women of different ages and cultural backgrounds to discuss and ask questions. Talking to other women can be of such great comfort and help. How do you think I gleaned all of these ideas? They didn't solely come from my brain or experience. So, call your mother, your sister, your girlfriend, your co-worker, your clergy; you name it! They will all have a different opinion or a story or two to share. We women mostly love to be helpful to one another and we all have something to give. However, you CANNOT share EVERYTHING!

Ladies, when you are in a relationship with a man; specifically, a serious relationship (i.e. long-term commitment, engagement or marriage), your deepest conversations need to be had with your partner and not with your 'Neighborhood Broadcasting System'. Men loathe when women *"put their business out there"*! Now...we've all heard men say this at some point; and true, some of them are excessive and go overboard with the whole 'privacy clause'. But you, ma'am, must learn to confide more in your partner and communicate your most intimate thoughts, issues and details to him. Unfortunately, if you are involved with an apathetical, detached, dispassionate man who doesn't seem to care, think about, or want to discuss anything with you; my friend, you, have another problem.

There are some very crucial reasons why this **"Thang"** can be very damaging and detrimental to the livelihood of your relationship. 1) It embarrasses the man because, most likely, it will get back to him some kind of way that you opened your mouth a tad bit too wide and usually in the wrong environment where his family members or his boys could hear. (*Now you, too, look stupid.*) 2) It shows your man that nothing is sacred or confidential when it comes to your relationship. In this instance, if *you* don't respect the sanctity and boundaries of your relationship, why should he? 3) Offering up too many details of personal intimacies and personal relationship facts WILL eventually lead you down a road of self-destruction. And don't bother blaming anyone but yourself because YOU opened that door. I said it was good to confer with other women but learn to *weed* through the advice and use what is applicable to you and your situation. You must never take the advice of other women completely verbatim and apply it to your own situation. It is absolute poison. No two men are alike; including father and son, OR identical twins! No two combinations of people breed the same results. The way you acted and behaved with your boo, Ralph, is not the same way you acted and behaved with your bae, James. Think about it! Do not take advice from mom, sister, cousins, and girlfriends; whether solicited or unsolicited, and apply it to your own relationship without filter. IT WILL NEVER WORK! You must tailor the advice to fit your own relationship. Remember, their advice is coming from their experience which may be similar or completely different than your own. It may also be coming from a place of bitterness. Be mindful of whom you share your info with and whom you accept advice from. People, in general, mean well; myself included, when they offer 'helpful advice'. But *"A wise woman builds her house, but with her own hands the foolish one tears hers down. A fool's mouth lashes out with pride, but the lips of the wise protect them."* – Proverbs 14:1, 3.

Other women will, if you allow them, tear down your house through you; whether they mean well or not. Some of them DO mean to tear it down because they want it for themselves. Beware: if you give someone the combination to your safe, don't be surprised to come home and find ALL your money gone! Nuf said...

Thang Number Six:
Never Be Insatiable; Be Satisfied

Let me just say, up front, that the only situation in which men happily accept an insatiable woman is in the bedroom. This does not apply to the insecure ones (alluded to in the men's section: **"Thang Number 8"**). Nothing pains, stresses and kills a man faster than an insatiable bi**h! Ooops! Did I say that word? Yes, I did! And here's why.

I once read a self-help book called: "Why Men Love Bi**hes" by Sherry Argov. And let me tell you, I learned a lot from what this sister (in the gender sense) had to say. 'Bi**h' in the context here means 'You don't walk over me'; 'I have a back bone'; or 'I won't stand for just any ol' thing you offer me'. The 'Bi**h' *I'm* referring to is the one who is the chronic whiner, complainer, beggar, etc. Let's look a bit deeper, shall we?

Men love to be praised as I said before. And no matter what your man does for you, whether it is a gesture of kindness or because it is the 'man' thang to do, *never* trivialize it! If he opens your door, say thank you. If he changes the light bulb, say thank you. When he pays for dinner, say thank you. If he washes your car, say thank you. You get my drift? Personally, I even thank my man for *being* my man. I know some of you will say, *"That is WAY too much, and he is only doing what he is supposed to do."* And you have a point, he is doing what he is supposed to do. However, how many frogs; I mean, men, have you dated before that were *supposed* to do something but never did it! Think back to how disappointing that was. How it made you feel frustrated or hurt; angry even. Just because someone is *supposed* to do something or is even *obligated* by marriage vows to do something doesn't mean that they will or even have to! If he said to you, *"You are my wife; you are* <u>*supposed*</u> *to cook me a hot meal every day!"* I don't think you'd appreciate that very much – at all! On the other hand, if he said, *"Honey, I know how tired you are but thank you so much for cooking me a hot meal today."* You would be grinning like the Cheshire Cat all day long and twice on Sunday! Everyone wants to feel appreciated and needed; not taken for granted. Men don't like the feeling that women feel as though something is 'their job'; even if it is. A job is something you get paid to do. A relationship is something you do because you want to; you choose to out of love, respect and adoration. Don't get it twisted! He may not comment when you go out and use his credit card without asking, knowing full well you have the money to cover your own shoe bill, but you use his because 'you can'. He may not say anything because you condescendingly expect him to always wash your car even though you don't bother to avoid the muddy route just because you know he likes for you to ride in a clean car. He may not say anything when you only want to have sex when it's convenient for you because it's 'your' body and he is supposed to be faithful, so you give it to him when 'you' want. He may not say, but eventually that silence turns deadly as well as turns his head to the one waiting in the wing who has mastered the art of stroking a man's ego. He will notice the woman who may not be as pretty as you, but she showers him with compliments simply because he opened her door or poured oil in her car. She didn't stick up her nose when they all went to lunch as co-workers and he offered to pay for her meal. She was grateful and ordered the grilled tuna sandwich instead of the most expensive thing on the menu because *he* was paying. He **will** notice her. She will become more desirable than you. Help your man, don't hinder him. If he can't afford those Red Bottoms but offered to buy the ones you saw in Aldo's, put a smile on your face and praise him for it! If you do...one day, he'll surprise you with those Red Bottoms long after you've forgotten. If you don't... ol' girl will be getting them...and much, much more...

Thang Number Seven:
Never Criticize His Sexual Skills

Oh lort! If you want to turn your man into the poster boy for the next mass murderer, talk about his penis in a negative way for an extended period of time. Run for cover! Ladies, PLEASE, PLEASE, PLEASE do NOT speak of your man's genitalia or sexual skills in a negative or derogatory manor in his face OR behind his back (please see the exposure statement in **"Thang Number Five"**). I know you sat here laughing when I characterized several types of poor male lovers in the man's section of **"Thang Number Eight"**. Heck, I laughed when I was writing it! But, oh boy, saying those things to him is prohibited! If your man classifies as any of those characters and you love him (if you don't – walk, end of story), this is the time to have those close intimate conversations I referred to in **"Thang Number Five"**. What it's NOT, is the time for you to be rude, selfish, patronizing, demeaning, humiliating... I think you know what I'm getting at.

A man is just that; a man. I don't care how much education he has, religion, class, age or the lack there of; a man identifies a great deal of himself by his penis and his skill level in using it. There, I said it! Every man, even the stank ones in **"Thang Number Eight"**, really wants to please his woman even if he does come off as a Neanderthal. Deep down, what he really wants is for his woman to be able to truthfully say that he has the biggest, the thickest, the longest, the most satisfying and the most skilled penis she has *ever* encountered (and there can be no more than one other past partner than him; but that's a whole other chapter so stay tuned)! *This* is the time to talk to him. Tell him what pleases you. Tell him what you like. If he's not listening, show him! But...you can't do that if you don't know ya darned self, now can you? Let me back up and take this step by step, because this lil culprit is DEFINITELY a relationship killer! (We're gonna take our time with this one.)

First off, ladies, how can you expect a man to know something that you don't even know? Some of you don't even know the proper names for your own body parts. You know the man's body parts better. So right there, you have set the standard that 'his' is more important than 'yours'. Think about it: growing up, it was called everything but what it really is! Cookie box, secret garden, nu-nu...now what on Earth is a 'nu-nu'? That works when you are five or six years old. However, some of you are 50 and 60 years old and *still* refer to your genitalia with these names! Sad, but true, you don't know the correct name yourself. Take some time to get to know yourself better (one famous comedian said); get naked in front of the mirror. Look at what you have, learn the names and then LEARN what makes it feel good! A man does not own a vagina and therefore cannot understand what to do to it to make it feel good OR take care of it. He must be taught. Even the best lovers still must be taught, because what works for you doesn't work for someone else. You can't be shy, nice-nasty or squeamish when it comes to sexuality but get mad cause the man 'always gets his' but you're left hanging. Hmmm, Yo fault! Fix this: first, fast and at last! Moving on...

When women do not address this situation, many times they end up 'Anita Fakers' (nothing against Anita, just a pun I heard on Martin once)! Whoooa! Your faking, ladies, is a flume ride to sexual hell for you AND your partner. You start faking to keep your relationship and you'll be faking your entire marriage to maintain it. He will never learn, and you will have created the worst sexual creature ever! *You* have led him to believe and trained him to think that he is "doing it right." You are every woman's worst nightmare because eventually they may end up with your 'Frankenstein Feel Good'.

Whenever I encounter a man who speaks as if he discovered the 'Dead Sea Vagina Scrolls', I have to try to control my involuntary eye rolling (which closely mirrors Linda Blair in the Exorcist). A man can be a great lover; even considered a connoisseur when it comes to sex. However, NO man is the author and finisher; the Alpha and Omega of coitus! Unless he has slept with every woman alive (which is quite a disgusting thought) and has catalogued and filed each case as well as memorized it; I assure you, he is *not* Adonis. This philosophy works both ways ladies. Don't assume that what you did for the last man will automatically satisfy the new one. It just doesn't work that way. God made each and every one of us different and that includes sexual difference. Don't be lazy! Take the time to ask and converse about what you like. I urge you to do it periodically in your relationship because things can change. What you or he liked two years ago may have evolved to something else or dropped off the charts altogether. Don't be impatient with yourself. Sometimes it takes a little concentration or practice to get used to or learn a new method of doing things. Make it fun and not a chore. Get him involved; he'll love it, I guarantee! Give him a score card; challenge him and yourself to improve each time. And most of all, be honest about how you feel. If he didn't get you there, tell him! Don't fake! Let him know what you need more of, or less of. Faking is not fair, and neither is criticizing his sex skills. Remember when I talked about your strengths as a woman? Well here it is again; now USE it! Negative reinforcement produces negative results. You'll never get where you need to be or what you want with verbal punishment. But what you will get is...a lifetime of self-induced hyperventilation!

Thang Number Eight:
Never Follow or Chase Him

Proverbs 18:22 says: *"He who finds a wife finds a good thing, and obtains favor from the Lord."* By now I'm sure that you have surmised, as you have been reading this book, that I have some level of deep seeded spirituality. This I won't deny. Everyone has a foundation; something to build on. Mine is spirituality and the Word of God. I include this rationalization because I understand that everyone is not (in their mind) a quote unquote 'spiritual' person. You don't have to be. That's your choice. All I want you to understand before I go forth in this chapter is that you must have some foundation whereby your principles lie. If you don't you are lost. My foundation happens to be a spiritual one. The passage states *"He who finds..."* and not *'she who finds'*. (There are lots of angry women right now.) I don't care! It is NOT your job to find a man. Let's look at the non-spiritual view. Men have always dominated in strength and physical stature in general. It is the man who approaches the tribe to name his intended bride. It is the man who solicits the father's blessing to date his daughter. Get this in your head and get it now: women *approve* but men *choose!* Stop wagging your finger and swirling your neck at me. Think about it...

You meet this guy and he's all that. You like him, go out with him, have sex with him, cook for him, wash for him, clean for him, and whatever else it is you do to (get this) make him *choose* you over all others. That's right. Most women would be married, there would be no 'single and suffering' syndromes and no out of wedlock children if women could choose. Women approve: we want him. Men choose: he wants you to be. Therefore, as a woman, you should never follow him (unjustifiably) or chase him. (Someone else is angry now.)

When I say, "don't follow or chase him", I am referring to these types of situations:

1. Guy is dating you. Guy is feeling you. Guy gets a new job. Guy relocates to another city or state. Guy does not ask you to marry him (choose you). Woman, do not follow him. Stay right where you are. If he wanted you to come with him or where he is, he would have *chosen* you. Here's another:

2. Guy is dating you. Guy is feeling you. Guy starts behaving different. Guy is seeing another woman. Guy lets you go for the other woman. Woman, do not chase him. Stay right where you are. If he wanted you, he would never have been with that other woman nor would he have left you for the 'whore' (I know that's how it feels) to begin with.

These are two *very* painful scenarios that many women, including myself, have faced. This is why I can tell you, ladies, following and chasing only further exacerbates the inevitable: HE DOESN'T WANT YOU! The man *must* choose you in order for the shopping at Tiffany's and Jared's to take place. It's tight but it's right! (Got that one from church too.) Now you may say to yourself, "*Where is my power in these situations? It seems*

I have no say and I am left at the mercy of the man; not fair!" You're right, it doesn't seem fair if you look at it that way. But here's another way to look at it: No matter how much you feel and think he is the one (even if he is behaving like he is), why on Earth would you want someone who doesn't see you as 'highly favored' enough to choose you over all others? Favor yourself! You know your worth. If he doesn't then perhaps it just isn't in the stars, or in God's plan. Again, the universe gives back what you give it. Trust it. Trust God. Go somewhere and cry and pull yourself together. But do not try to follow, chase, force, manipulate, cajole, bargain, compromise or use any other negotiation tactic to get him to choose you. He must do this on his own. You want him to do it on his own. Remember, you were made in God's image and God gives us the option to choose. He is not a dictator or manipulator. He wants us to do things because it's right and because we want to. Who wants someone's unrequited love? Not I! And neither do you...really. Don't let your emotions and feelings of inadequacy be the driving force of your relationship with any man. You want someone who will reciprocate your love. You want someone who freely and willingly wants you to be by his side; to be his wife. Nothing less. Don't settle for: long term girlfriend, live in partner, baby love, boo... DO NOT compromise what you want, but DO NOT force it either. I know the pain you face. I know the rejection, the inadequate feeling of not being good enough, the "what's wrong with me" syndrome. There is nothing wrong with you. Love must happen on its own. It must be left the freedom to choose. It is the most powerful emotion. Trust it. Trust your gut. Trust God. You can't lose; you won't lose. You will win every time. But you will surely lose if you follow and pressure. Your gain will be only temporary and then it will fade away. You will point fingers and place blame. You are to blame. Remember this: only follow God; only follow His Word; only follow your heart (aligned with the Word). You will receive all that you've dreamed of. Follow a man for love's sake, and you will end up on an aimless, pointless road to emotional destruction and disappointment. You are a queen; act and behave accordingly.

Thang Number Nine:
Never Be Helpless

Oh, here comes those darned Turner Classic Network movies again (I still love you, TCN, you have your purpose too). But the times have changed. If you've attended church I'm sure you've heard this: *"The Word of God is the same, it never changes"*. It doesn't! But let me clarify some things here. The Word of God (principles) *don't* change and are still relevant today. However, the era and the time when it was written has changed and will continue to do so. Times are supposed to change, and we must change with it to remain relevant. Helplessness in a woman is no longer relevant. There is no need for you to revert to the 'I can't do it, I'm a woman' web of deceit. That's right, it's a web of deceit. Herein lies a fine line, ladies, of being a woman and being a lady. A woman is strong and resilient. She can do mostly anything she puts her mind to. She is not helpless. She is not unlearned. She is not a legendary damsel in distress. Helen Reddy sang: *"I am woman hear me roar. In numbers too big to ignore. And I know too much to go back an' pretend. Cause I've heard it all before. And I've been down there on the floor. No one's ever going to keep me down again. Oh, yes, I'm wise. But it's wisdom born of pain. Yes, I've paid the price. But look how much I've gained. If I have to, I can do anything. I am strong. I am invincible. I am woman!"* Roar, ladies! You can do it! Whatever it is, you can. The alternative question is: *"Should you"*? Ladies know what they should and should not do; even if they can. You may be capable, as a woman, but as a lady, determine what you should do when it comes to being with a man and in a relationship. Let me explain...

Women who came before you have fought so hard to gain equality. They have fought for the right: to choose, to work, to give birth or not, to make decisions, to handle finances and business affairs and sing about it! (Helen Reddy; look her up). And we are good at it (some of us, anyway). The 'pretend' damsel in distress is disgusting and distasteful for other women to witness and a complete menace for men to encounter. Yea, yea, yea, I know you've been told that men like to feel needed and you need to 'act' like you need them, so you play dumb and helpless. Do you really think men are that stupid? (I'm speaking up for you, men.) Men (most of them) can spot a fake a mile away. Helpless you may seem. Intrigued he may be. He may even appear to like it because he feels empowered; like a MAN. Honey, if he's a *real* man, he doesn't need you to behave like a weak bubble head to make him feel like one! This, too, will only last for a short while. He will get tired of your needy behavior; your whining; your cumbersome dependence. You have gone from TCN's damsel in distress to the SyFy's dragon of duress; a lame liability! You are like a dead weight to your man. You are not a biblical help mate. You are a diabolical burden! You can wash your own car. You can take out the trash. You can earn your own keep. You can do all of that; and you should. Let your man know that you are fully capable. He will appreciate the gesture as well as the effort. BUT, if the trash is awkward and heavy, ask him to help you with it! I guarantee he will smile and take the whole thing off your hands (and probably ask if there's anything else you need help with). If your car is dirty, wash it. He will see you doing that and if for no other reason, take over the job (he doesn't want other men to see you washing your car; it's not manly). Listen, ladies, there's a delicate balance here. Learn to decipher when, where, how, and why. No man wants to feel like he has 'Vera de Milo' or 'The Incredible Hulk' for a wife or partner. At the same time, you cannot act and behave like an amoeba either (just existing). Men, like women, appreciate the effort and willingness to try and learn. They realize you can't do certain things or that you are limited to perform certain tasks. But it's a whole different ball game for a woman that knows she can't but gives her all to try anyway than a woman who just 'assigns' the duty to you and doesn't try or care. Be proactive. You like it when he takes it upon himself to make dinner, clean, or perform other duties that you normally take on. Why wouldn't he appreciate the same? Helplessness is a fast track to nowhere! Ask yourself this question: *"Who would do it if he weren't there? Who would take care of it if he died?"* Learn how to do, even if you physically can't. At least when you hire someone, you'll know if they're doing it right. No need to take your man's place 'being manly' or 'being the man'. However, no need to allow him to assume responsibility for every little thing either. If you do, get ready for some real-life dictatorship in your relationship! The anarchy will spread to every aspect of your life with him...even to the bedroom (see the Men's section **"Thang Number Eight"**)! Helpless evolves to HOPELESS...quickly!

Thang Number Ten:
Never Overstay Your Welcome
(Know When to Walk Away)

My dear mother always had a saying (as most folks' moms did). She'd tell me: *"You don't want to wear out your welcome!"* I thought that odd, as a young girl. If one is welcome, how can one wear it out? Listen up...

Suppose you invite your friend over for a visit. You think he/she is only going to be around for a couple of hours. Five hours later after you have run out of beer, toilet paper, snacks and patience; you are trying to figure out a way to put them out graciously (unless you're Martin Lawrence). This is a scenario of someone who has worn out their welcome! That's the simplistic version. Let's take a look at the relationship version...

You are dating this guy. It starts out subtle (as often, it does). You go out; you go home. You go over to visit (invited); you go back home. Now follow this paradigm: he doesn't invite you over again (in the time frame that you wanted or expected). You call him to invite yourself. (NO!) You show up as if you are an undercover CIA agent. (NO!) You keep hinting around every time you speak with him. (NO!) You put his number on redial (since it mysteriously keeps going to voice mail). No, No, NO!!! Can you see how 'wearing out your welcome' can become closely related to stalking? Welcome can quickly turn into 'Come, well...?' Even if you felt or thought that y'all were having a wonderful time, you must wait for the follow up invitation. You must be patient and quiet. But you must not incite the invitation and you most certainly may not just show up! Climbing trees and hanging on branches trying to see what or whom he is doing in his private quarters is strictly prohibited. This is what Michael Baisden is referring to when he comically repeats, *"Crazy...deranged!"* Ladies, please re-read the Women's section **"Thang Number Eight"**. While you're at it, re-think what I said about wearing that orange jump suit and Chanel bracelets. If a man enjoys your company, trust your own worth; he will invite you again (and you should not always accept, but that's a whole other topic). Sometimes when you are visiting, cut it short. Leave early. Go home! Men are funny creatures. They bask in the notion that they have your attention, you are available, and you are fun to be with (providing that you are). However, the tables will turn quickly if you offer too many treats, too often and too soon. They will get bored and annoyed very quickly and you won't even know why. It's because, you have worn out your welcome. The novelty has died. You are old news. And no longer welcome. Go to your mom's house, your girl's house, your neighbor's house, the house of wax, the house of God, YOUR OWN HOUSE! Go HOME! Do not linger around a man all the time. You will wear out your welcome! Now let's turn the tables and talk about 'knowing when to walk away...'

I think we can cover this with minimal sentences, don't you? Let's see... If a man is repeatedly unkind in any way: walk away. If a man is cheating: (particularly more than once; that means 2 times, ladies) walk away (I believe in forgiveness and second chances in certain circumstances). If a man puts his hands on you other than to pray for you, protect you, or profess his love for you intimately: walk away (do not pass go, or wait for the 2nd time in this case); as a matter of fact, RUN AWAY! Let's remove the violence, because some of you still don't get it. Even if a man is kind and great in terms of your expectations but he continues to show signs of being a pedophile or any other unpleasantry: walk away. It is not your job to fix anyone. You cannot fix a person. You cannot 'train' a man, in this sense. He is not a circus animal. He is a person. A creation of God. If God doesn't fix it (and He won't if He's not invited to) *you* certainly cannot. Do not take on this task. You are wasting your time and his! If you are already married to a man, walking away can prove to be difficult in many situations. However, difficult is not synonymous with impossible. *"You gotta know when to hold 'em; know when to fold 'em; know when to walk away; know when to RUN!"* You don't even listen to country music, but you already knew that verse came from Kenny Rogers. Ladies, we are fighters. We fight for what we want and what we believe in; and for whom we love. But you need to know when to walk away AND when to run. The most important person in your relationship is YOU. You must remain whole. You must remain a commodity. Your time and attention are priceless. But he won't know or realize that if you're always shoving it down his throat. And you will lose your worth AND yourself if you continue to force yourself or your presence upon any one (re-read **"Thang Number Nine"**). It's okay and downright honorable to walk away. Failure starts with failing yourself! So, if you find yourself in an 'unfavorable relationship' for any reason that is not healthy to you: walk away. Tomorrow will still come if he is not there. I promise you, it will...

Thang Number Eleven:
Never Disrespect Him

I believe in my audience; my readers. I assume that they are all intelligent to some extent. You don't have to be Einstein to observe that this last chapter has the same title as the last chapter for the men. It's called: reinforcement. Disrespect is one of my all-time pet peeves. I literally hold it with the utmost disdain. Why? Because it is foul, self-degrading and unnecessary. You do not need to ever revert to disrespect. Walk away (see **"Thang Number Ten"**). If you are in a relationship or dating a man and you ever get the inkling for a need to disrespect him, LEAVE! That's right, leave before you revert to disrespect. Why stay? The relationship is done anyway. *"But he is disrespectful to me!"* you whine. **"Thang Number Three"**, aw heck, just re-read the whole book! No one does anything to you lest you allow it. Retaliation is not biblical nor profitable. Do not hit your man (see how I'm repeating myself). Do not manipulate. Do not play the 'I'm gonna make you jealous' game. Do not curse him out because he didn't show up or call. Do not shamelessly flirt, ignore, or treat him as an afterthought. If he 'deserves it', there is your reason to walk away. Again, this behavior is not only a waste of time but dangerous. Face it: no woman wants a man she can 'run over'. We no longer see him as 'a man' but rather as 'a pair of pants' (that's another one of my mom's favorites). Who needs 'a pair of pants'? You have several in your own closet. A real woman desires a real man (I'm speaking as a heterosexual). Take that title away and all you've got is 'a pair of pants'. You may be angry. You may even be justified. But you'd better be careful. You could end up at that Mac counter again. He is a man. Allow him to be. Do not attempt to remove that title with unsavory words or behavior. If he is behaving as less than a man, then walk away (**"Thang Number Ten"**) and leave him to figure out the path back to manhood. You can't teach him anyway; you know nothing about what it is to be a man. It's not your job. You will be unfulfilled. God gave us roles as men and women. Stay in your lane. Stand up for yourself; roar (as a woman). You can do it. Use your female talents; your womanly ways; your thinking and reasoning abilities. Any man will tell you that a woman can out think a man. He knows! He is a man and he knows his role, his talents and his lane. Know yours! Disrespect is never necessary nor is it smart. It will end your relationship bitterly, if you're lucky, because it could end your life!

Bonus Chapter:
Save Some for *Jesus!*

That's right! Even the 'non-spiritual' readers can agree with this one. Save some for Jesus. *"Whatever do you mean, Black Mermaid?"* I'll tell you... remember that word – tell...

Ladies and gentlemen, this chapter is a bonus for both men and women. When you meet someone, it's exciting. When you're attracted you really want to get to know that person more. You want to know all their favorite things, what they don't like, what their dreams and aspirations are... You want to know all you can...or do you?

It's fine to get to know someone. Heck, it's a requirement! However, it is not necessary to address things that are deeply personal – and not really your business! I have a motto: Aside from knowing your HIV status, if it happened circa BM (Before Me) it is not my business and you can tell me at your own discretion (I may even stop you mid-sentence if I see where it is going. I don't wanna know!) That's right! I am not interested in analyzing how many sexual partners he's had prior to me. If he's clean, healthy and I like him, who gives a rat's behind. Why do I care? Unless he's struggling with his sexual identity i.e. whether or not he's gay, I have no right to probe or demand answers about his sexual prowess (or the lack thereof). I always felt it mighty bold for a man to ask me the number of sexual partners I've had. Why is that any of his business? What will he gain by hearing me say "2" or "20"? Nothing but information he really didn't want or need to know. Is he asking because he wants to judge me? Is he asking because he wants to 'gain some insight' on my character or personality? Is he asking to impose a double standard? Let's face it, as I said earlier, for a woman, NO number 0 to 9 (that includes all digits that are made up of these base ones) is safe! One other is one too many. He really doesn't want to hear it. He wants to know, and he doesn't. Men and women, ask yourself why this is important. I also operate under the rule of: Don't ask what you really don't want to know. I would suggest you add this to your rule book, ye daters. Before you pose a question to your date, your partner, your husband, your wife; ask yourself: Do you really *need* to know? Do you really *want* to know? Can you *handle* the answer? These questions are vital and require mental exploration *prior* posing random questions for lack of other topics to discuss. Some things are shameful to others and they would rather not share. Your date may be 40 years old and a virgin. Your date may be 25 and had a sordid past. Your partner could have experienced rape or molestation. Try to focus more on what attracted you in the first place and glean from that. If you continue your relationship and it grows stronger, that person may opt to open up and tell you things...things that they had opted to *save* for Jesus. Remember, they are sharing with you because they have come to trust you. Somethings need to be left unsaid. Somethings need to be left for God alone! It's not always something reprehensible, but sometimes simply uncomfortable. That is the quickest way to turn a person off; asking questions that – as my husband says - you have no clearance for! (Ha! I love it!) You have <u>no</u> clearance. You have no need to know every little detail about a person's life. Leave that to God. Let Jesus hold somethings for you. Probing in uncharted areas can prove to be quite dangerous and damaging to a relationship. Women, I'm talking to you as well. Listen, people, don't ask things like: Who was better in bed? Who was a better cook? or Have you ever...? You know that game. I'm not talking about have you ever been to London, either. Just grow up, for crying out loud! Anyone who has reached the age of legitimate dating has accounts, stories, ideas, and experiences. Some of them are good and some of them are bad; AND some of them are very bad! But if the person has learned from them (see, this is the key); learned from their experiences, their mistakes, their bad choices; then you, my friend, have encountered the best of them so far! Do not pressure someone to discuss something they are uncomfortable with. On the other hand, do not offer up unsolicited information (unless you have good reason). No one wants to hear how you single-handedly conquered 1,000 women in less than two years! No one wants to hear that you only slept with one man – your best friend's father! No one wants to hear that 'Sheila' gave the best head ever! I think you get my point. Save some for Jesus. Even after you've gained clearance, tread lightly, please. Sticks and stones may break your bones, but words are unforgettably hurtful. Shhhh! Be quiet, and **save some for JESUS!**

Summary

I truly hope that you have enjoyed this book as much as I have enjoyed writing it. I've listened to a lot of people over the course of my life. They have offered me unsolicited information and asked for my unsolicited opinions and advice. Many times, I was taken aback because it was a stranger, or someone I hardly knew. Sometimes it was someone I knew very well and they (for whatever reason) decided to confide in me. I finally stopped running from it. I wanted to help in any way that I could. Am I an expert? I think not! But somewhere, somehow, these people thought enough of me and my character to open up to me. And I appreciate each and every one of you who did. I learned a lot! I listened, and I applied those things, scenarios, and thoughts to my own life. As I've said before, you don't always have to experience something first hand to learn from it. Learn from other peoples' mistakes. Try not to judge them; and if you must, keep it to yourself! I want everyone to find happiness in their romantic life. It is important. So important, God put a drive between both our legs that is unprecedented! He meant for us to love and marry. No one wants to be alone; not really. God didn't intend for it to be that way. So, if you're single, take these principles that I have given you and consider it while you are out there dating. If you are married, it's not too late to change! Change your mind, your behavior, your attitude. It will change your marriage. If not, you may need to consider other alternatives, i.e. counseling, marriage retreats, etc. I will never tell someone they need to get a divorce. That's not my call. You must make these decisions for yourself. But I will say, choose life! It's short and not promised. Dating, relationships and marriage can be fun and fulfilling. It's all in what you make it. But remember: There are just a few **Thangs** you should aught not do!

Acknowledgements

I would like to thank God for giving me the talent to express myself verbally and on paper. I never really considered it a big deal until my husband and other close friends of mine continued to confirm that clear communication is not a given. So, I thank God for such a talent and ability. I pray He continue to increase my skills for the edification of His people.

I would also like to thank my parents. Lawd knows they didn't ask for such a cantankerous child! But they stuck with it in spite of. To my father, now deceased, a bright eyed and bushy tailed character was he. Optimism was his specialty along with a love of people. At least, that's the way I viewed him. To my mother, strong and resilient. She had her way of getting things done! I think the Capricorn in her had something to do with that. To my step-father, whom is always referred to as "daddy", a much quieter man that never seemed to pass judgment on me a day in his life!

Finally, I pay homage to a host of family, friends, acquaintances, co-workers and strangers all of whom helped to make this possible. They shared stories and ideas with me that will give me fuel to write for the rest of my life! I've spent many hours laughing and crying with them all. I'd like to think that they learned a thing or two from me as well. We all have something to contribute and you should never ever hold back vital information that could help to make someone else's life better. Cheers to everyone! And keep talking!

CPSIA information can be obtained
at www.ICGtesting.com
Printed in the USA
FSOW02n1502130218
44278FS